When Life Throws You a Curveball

What to Do After You've Been in a Serious Accident

William Franchi

What to Do After You've Been in a Serious Accident

Disclaimer

This publication is designed to provide accurate and authoritative information regarding the subject matter contained within. It should be understood that the author and publisher are not engaged in rendering legal, accounting or other financial service through this medium. The author and publisher shall not be liable for your misuse of this material and shall have neither liability nor responsibility to anyone with respect to any loss or damage caused, or alleged to be caused, directly or indirectly by the information contained in this book. The author and/or publisher do not guarantee that anyone following these strategies, suggestions, tips, ideas or techniques will become successful. If legal advice or other expert assistance is required, the services of a competent professional should be sought.

ISBN-13: 978-1-946203-63-2

Expert Press

www.ExpertPress.net

Table of Contents

INTRODUCTION

You've been in a serious accident. You're hurt, your car may be totaled, and you don't know what to do. You don't see a way back to health and the life you were living before someone hit you.

I know what it's like for an accident to come out of nowhere and derail your life. In some ways, my whole life has been defined by such accidents.

I might still be a deputy at the Hillsborough County Sheriff's office if it wasn't for an accident. I might be a college baseball coach if not for an accident.

Accidents have changed the course of my life over and over again. But I know the secret to getting back on your feet and fighting back.

And I've put those secrets in this book.

Baseball Dreams

Before I'd ever dreamed of being a lawyer, all I'd ever wanted to be was a baseball player or a baseball coach.

Baseball is what brought me to Tampa. The University of Tampa represented a chance for a new beginning after a couple unsuccessful years at the University of Western Carolina. I'd ended up at Western Carolina because my dad's best friend—former professional baseball player, Scooter Gay—was an alumnus. I grew up idolizing Scooter, and I figured if he could make a baseball career out of that school, so could I.

It didn't work out that way. So, the Thanksgiving of my junior year, I went down to Tampa to meet with baseball coach Joe Urso. After speaking with him, he didn't make any big promises. All he told me was, "We'll give you a shot, it's up to you what you do with it."

But that's all I needed.

Urso reignited my passion for baseball and gave me a path back to my dream career: coaching at the college level.

Then, only two weeks into my time at Tampa, I suffered my first big injury. I was warming up in the bullpen when something in my arm just didn't feel right. It started to ache to the point I couldn't throw at all.

I went to have an MRI, and it showed that I had torn my ulnar collateral ligament. To fix it, I had to have what's called Tommy John surgery, named after the famous pitcher.

The reconstruction, unfortunately, was not a success. And so, there went all my baseball dreams. Lost to an accident.

Keep Swinging

I never got my pitching arm back, but I wasn't going to give up so easily. After my surgery, I went through a year of rehab. When it became clear I would never be able to pitch in a game again, I kept contributing to the team in every way I could. As soon as I could throw more than five feet, I helped the team by pitching for fly balls during practice.

Then, when I graduated, I picked up the pieces, and I took my life in a new direction: the sheriff's office.

For a few years, it looked like I'd fallen into a promising new career, but it all went wrong again with a foot chase on another Thanksgiving.

I was patrolling a neighborhood that had some drug problems. It was about 3:00 AM, and I saw a guy on a bike whom I didn't know. Now, it was my job to protect that neighborhood from violence, and part of that job was getting to know everyone in that community.

I knew that area well, and the guy riding by on his bike, I didn't know him. So, I made the decision to stop him.

I turned my lights on. The curb was too high for the cruiser. I knew, if he stayed on the bike, I couldn't catch him. If he stopped, I wouldn't need to run. But, if he got off the bike and ran, I'd have to give chase.

And run is precisely what he did. I might have caught him and kept my career on the path I'd set it, except there was a storm drain in the road that I couldn't see in the dim light. I stepped down into that drain and twisted my right leg. I did a Pete Rose slide across the street.

I got up, dusted myself off, and looked around. The guy was gone, and so—although I didn't know it yet—was my career.

After a couple months hoping the injury would take care of itself, I went to the doctor, had another MRI, and found out I needed hip surgery.

Just like the Tommy John surgery before, I never fully recovered. I spent a few months on light duty behind a desk, but it was clear by then I was never getting back on the streets.

These injuries destroyed my dreams about my future. When it became too painful to pitch, it became too painful to stick with baseball. When it became too painful to run, it became too painful to call myself a deputy when I couldn't do the street work.

But I don't believe in giving up when things get tough. I believe you have to keep swinging, even if you have to adjust what you're swinging for.

"It's Up to You What You Do with It"

After each of these incidents, Coach Urso's words came back to me. I still had a shot, but it was up to me to do something with it.

After you've been in an accident, you can feel like you don't have any options. You've medical bills, pain, trouble getting to work and doing your work. You may have a car that needs repairs. In such moments, it can seem that all your choices have been taken off the table. You just want to get better, but you don't see a way to do it.

But I can tell, I've lived through it, and you can come back from this. You can get better. You can move on from this.

You do have a shot. And once you see that, you can decide whether you want to take it.

To get back to living your life, you're going to need help. You're going to need guidance and support, and you're probably going to need a lawyer.

I've written this book as a way to help you start healing and moving your life forward again. Whether you've been in an accident or you just want to be prepared if the worst ever happens, within these pages, you'll learn what you're up against and how you can come out on top.

This is your shot to get your life back. I hope you take it.

Part I

The Curveball

Chapter 1

Accidents Throw Your Whole Life a Curveball

Last fall, seventeen-year-old Stacy Trent was just another passenger in a car out on a rural road, out having fun after cheerleading practice. I'm sure, on that afternoon, she didn't have a worry in the world…or no worry beyond those of a typical teenager.

That all changed when a woman ran a stop sign and crashed right into the passenger side of Stacy's car. In an instant, Stacy's life—and the life of her parents—was torn apart.

The crash was serious. The car was half-obliterated, and it took the jaws of life to get Stacy out. She was taken to the emergency room, where doctors had to perform emergency surgery and remove her spleen.

She survived, but her life was still going to be dramatically different. Her injuries were still serious. In particular, she had lost the use of one of her arms because of severe nerve damage.

To recover, Stacy had to put aside a senior year that was meant to be full of fun memories she'd cherish forever.

She quit cheerleading to focus on her rehab and recovery. At the same, her parents—who hadn't been on speaking terms—had to find a way to communicate because neither of them had the money to cover all their new medical bills.

It could have gone wrong quickly for them, but thankfully, Stacy's father came to me, and we were able to make sure the family got the compensation they needed, so that Stacy could get to rehab and get better and the family could avoid bankruptcy.

The accident meant she would miss out on being a senior cheerleader, but because of that settlement, she's now recovered the use of her arm, and she's getting ready to go to college this fall.

Accidents come out of nowhere and profoundly change your life, as well as the lives of those you love. They can destroy all that is precious to you: your health, your well-being, your access to medicine, your savings, your transportation, your work, and your belief that life can get better.

Your accident has disrupted your life. You don't need a book to tell you that. But before I can help you find the way back, we need to talk about just what you're up against.

Finding a Doctor

Usually, when we're hurt, our first instinct is to go to our primary care physician (PCP). After all, we know that doctor, and they know us. We trust their judgment and expect them to heal us.

Unfortunately, most PCPs won't see patients who have been in accidents. I don't want to say your doctor definitely won't see you, but the odds are not in your favor.

Instead, when you show up at your doctor's office, you are far more likely to be flat-out told they can't help. They may recommend somebody else, but they aren't required to. They may just tell you to go to the emergency room.

This is a problem, even if you feel your injuries aren't serious. Often, what might seem like a bit of back pain may prove to be something quite serious. A headache may prove to be a concussion. Even a so-called "minor" crash can require surgery and may result in years of pain.

If you can't get to a doctor, how can you know the extent of your injuries? And, whether those injuries are serious or slight, temporary or long-term, you need proper care to make a full recovery.

Now, I don't know if PCPs do this because they don't feel equipped to deal with the injuries you're suffering from or because they don't want to get involved in a potential lawsuit. In the end, it doesn't matter. Your doctor probably won't help you, so you're going to have to find someone else.

One of the main reasons people come to lawyers like me after an accident is because lawyers tend to know doctors who will take care of patients after an accident.

Getting Around

Tampa is not an easy city to get around without a vehicle. The city and surrounding area is far too spread out to accommodate much use of bikes or walking, and our public transportation options just aren't reliable enough when you need to get to work or a doctor's appointment on time.

So, if your car has been totaled in an accident, you've really got no choice but to get it fixed and get it fixed immediately. Unfortunately, as we'll discover, Florida law doesn't make it easy to navigate your insurance to get your vehicle fixed. When you don't have enough money on hand to handle the repairs on your own, this can become a terrible dilemma.

Getting Back to Work

Whether you have your car or not, you may still be dealing with difficulties getting to work and making money. After all, not every job is able to accommodate the massive disruption that an accident makes in someone's life.

Not all jobs come with enough sick leave to cover the time it takes to fix a car and recover sufficiently from an accident. And often, those same jobs aren't able to accommodate the hours you need off to visit your doctor.

But even if your job does have those benefits—even if you are able to get leave, fix your car, and get to the doctor—coming back may still not be a realistic option.

Many labor jobs require lifting. But what do you do when your doctor tells you that you can't bend and lift repeatedly anymore?

What do you do when your traumatic brain injury makes it impossible to think in the way your job requires?

Whether you know it or not, this accident may be the end of your career as you know it. In the same way my foot chase incident ended my career as a deputy, you may find yourself needing to find a new way to make money and support your family.

I once helped an electrician named Ben who had been in a "minor" car accidents. After the crash, he could still do the technical side of his job, but there were physical aspects to his work that he'd never considered before. To rewire homes, he had to be able to move around, bend down, and get into tight spaces. And that was simply no longer possible.

Ben had been doing this work for as long as he could remember. He was a trained expert with more than a decade of experience.

But he simply couldn't do it anymore. He had to transition into a desk job in an unrelated field. Now, we got him a settlement that helped him in that transition, but that's the kind of massive life change these accidents can throw at you.

The Other Big Questions

This is just the start for most people who are dealing with one of life's biggest curveballs. Every day, I have people who come into my office who want to know all of the above, and also...

- How do I tackle everyday activities like getting up and down the stairs or going to the bathroom?
- How do I find the time to get well when I have so many bills to worry about?
- How do I deal with this complicated insurance stuff?
- How will I get the money to put my life back together?
- How is this ever going to be okay?

We're going to work through all of these questions in the book. The fact is, this stuff is tough. It's hard. The road back to health and happiness isn't easy. Trust me, I've walked it a number of times.

But with the right guidance, and the right help, there is a way back.

Sometimes, life throws you a curveball, but with the right advice and the right people on your side, there is way to knock it out of the park.

Chapter 2

The Risks of the Road

In my opinion, Tampa is the best city in the world, but that doesn't mean it doesn't have risks, particularly on the road. You can be doing everything right and still end up in a catastrophic accident.

I once represented a woman, whom I'll call Tammy Reese to protect her identity, who was a successful small-town politician with ambitions for running for major office. She was in her fifties, healthy, charismatic, and quite popular with her constituency. Everything looked like it was going her way.

That is, until a tractor-trail ran right into her.

Tammy was on the way home from work when it happened. She was doing everything right, driving at a safe speed on her regular route. It was raining, and ahead of her was a ramp with a particularly big curve. On that ramp was a truck with an empty trailer flying towards her. Now, that driver should have taken a sharp curve on a rainy day with an empty trailer slowly. But he didn't.

He crashed into Tammy going well over the speed limit and pushed her car into a pond. The car began to submerge. Luckily, the emergency medical services arrived in time to pull her out. The truck driver, meanwhile, was mostly concerned about the whereabouts of his Bluetooth earpiece.

Tammy's life was completely wrecked that day. She had a traumatic brain injury that made it hard for her to do basic daily activities like laundry and feeding her dogs, let alone taking care of her elected office. She ended up retiring shortly afterwards.

You can imagine, when Tammy came to me, how a case like that made me feel. A brilliant politician reduced to early retirement by a truck driver who didn't even care what he'd done.

That was why I decided not just to go for compensatory damages that would cover her bills and care, but for punitive damages to make that driver pay.

To get those damages, I had to go up against the main partner at one of Florida's biggest defense firm. This was the guy they sent out for trials and motion hearings on big cases. It came down to him and me, and he had precedent on his side. Florida courts don't like giving out punitive damages on truck accidents. All he had to do was argue that this case was like any other.

That didn't stop me, though. I used the facts of the case to win Tammy punitive damages that took her final settlement from $700,000 to $1,200,000. Enough for Tammy to put her life back together as best she could.

Tammy was doing everything right in her life. She was an excellent public servant and a careful driver. But that didn't save her from the thoughtless actions of a truck driver.

That can happen to any of us, even in a safe, wonderful community like Tampa. The best protection we can have against such accidents is to know the risks now, so we can always know what to do if the worst happens to us.

Car Accidents

Car accident cases are perhaps the most straightforward from a legal perspective. While there are always exceptions, on average, the injuries in car-on-car accidents are less severe than those in the other types of accidents we'll look at below.

Your four-way stop, ten-mile-an-hour crash rarely results in the kind of injuries we see with pedestrians or trucks, for example. And that means the stakes are lower and the case is easier to resolve.

Usually, we can get most of the information we need from your car's black box. You may not realize it, but the vast majority of cars on the road now have recorders which capture everything about the car. Black box information, combined with witnesses, police reports, and sometimes recorded footage or pictures, usually allows us to put the case together relatively quickly and inexpensively.

Of course, all that changes with catastrophic car accidents. With those cases, things are much closer to the other kinds of accidents I describe below.

Pedestrian and Bicycle Accidents

The most distinct difference between most car-on-car accidents and all the rest that will follow is the seriousness of the injuries.

When a vehicle hits a pedestrian or a bicyclist, there's so much more risk for injury. In fact, generally, these accidents are either fatal or at least debilitating.

Relatively unique to this type of accident is the hit-and-run risks. Of course, we see hit-and-runs from other types of accidents, but they are more common with pedestrians and bicyclists.

We recently resolved just such a case. A driver hit a pedestrian, Maxwell Harris. Maxwell was one of the lucky ones, and his injuries weren't that serious, but that didn't stop the person behind the wheel from driving away and leaving Maxwell to take care of himself.

To make matters worse, this driver was a doctor. He had a pretty nasty driving record, including a felony for drunk driving. True to form, we believed he was drunk again, which was why he fled to his office. That's where the police found him.

Still, even with this doctor obfuscating, we were able to establish fault, and we made sure Maxwell's medical bills were completely covered.

Not every case goes as smoothly as Maxwell's. On such cases, it's important to always bring a lawyer in who knows how to best tackle catastrophic injury and hit-and-run tactics.

Motorcycle Accidents

Like pedestrian and bicycle accidents, motorcycle crashes are often fatal. When they aren't, they still result in very serious injuries, particularly to the brain and spine.

More unique to motorcycle accidents is the potential need for plastic surgery. Road rash, where the skin scrapes against the pavement, can require significant skin repairs and skin grafts.

We also see a lot of orbital fractures—that's the bone right around your eye. If you hit your face on the pavement, it typically breaks. We've seen multiple clients that required surgery, mesh, and plastic surgery to repair that area.

That's not to say that all motorcycle accidents are necessarily catastrophic. We recently resolved a motorcycle case where our client, like Maxwell, was extremely lucky. He had no broken bones, minor injuries, and minimal hospital bills. He missed some work to recover from the bumps and bruises, but was otherwise back on his feet pretty quickly.

So, these accidents do run the whole gamut, but most of the time, they're quite serious.

Truck Accidents

Truck accidents have their own separate level of complexity and destruction. When a truck collides with a vehicle, it is almost always extremely serious, as we saw in Tammy's case.

At the same time, truck accidents also usually involve big companies with big insurance policies and big money to spend on big lawyers to defend themselves against claims. That means there's a lot more work on the legal end for your case.

There's also more technical complexity in these cases. While most cars have black boxes, some trucks actually have two of them.

One of those black boxes is very similar to the one in cars, and to interpret that information, you can use local experts. The other black box, though, can only, usually, be downloaded and reviewed by experts in two locations in the entire country. On the East Coast, that location is in North Carolina.

That means, to move a trucking case forward, we have to fly somebody in from North Carolina.

The logistics would be tough enough on their own, but trucking companies aren't interested in making it any easier for us.

We have an on-going case at the moment in just that predicament. It involves an entire family. They were all in the car—mother, father, and two toddlers—when a truck hit them. All of them suffered severe injuries.

To make this case, we needed to get the information from that second black box, but the trucking company didn't want to play ball. They told us they wanted to get the truck back out on the road in the next couple days, and they weren't going to wait for the experts to show up and get the data.

We couldn't get the people down from North Carolina before the trucking company's deadline, so instead, we went ahead and filed the lawsuit right away, with an emergency injunction to keep that truck off the road. The judge took our side, and we were able to keep that truck out of service until we could get the people from North Carolina flown in.

All Accidents Are the Same

In the end, while these accidents can all be very different from an injury and legal standpoint, from your perspective, they are all essentially the same.

You've been hurt, you have medical bills you shouldn't have to pay, and your life has been turned upside down. Whether it's from a car or truck, whether you were on foot or behind the wheel, you need to make sure you are getting the right assistance so you get fair compensation while attempting to pull your life back together.

Chapter 3

Your Immediate Response to an Accident

We recently had a client—Dave Schepp—who came to us worrying about whether he could paid his hospital bills. He had been in a car accident, and his insurance company had taken it upon themselves to settle his medical bills up to that point.

Great, we said, that sounds like a real help, but the fact is, the insurance company had told Dave that now they'd paid those first bills, they weren't going to cover anything else.

Dave had recovered from his most serious injuries, but he still had a lot of pain issues, and he was afraid that he was going to have to either pay for further treatment himself or simply go without.

Thankfully, Dave never signed anything from the insurance company, and as soon as he started getting pushed around, he came directly to us. Because of that, we were able to make sure the insurance covered all of his bills, not just the ones they wanted to cover.

We were able to take care of Dave because he knew what to do when things went wrong. Unfortunately, most people don't realize it, but what they do in the immediate minutes, hours, and days after an accident can determine whether they get the compensation they need to get healthy and avoid major bills.

So, if things ever go wrong for you, follow all of the advice in this chapter to protect yourself.

Take Care of Your Health First

Your health and the health of others involved in the accident is your highest concern. If you have any inkling that you are hurt, call emergency services. In fact, call regardless, since they will send police who will help record what happened.

Also, don't assume just because you don't feel hurt right away that you aren't really hurt.

After a crash, you're not necessarily in the right state of mind to ascertain whether you've suffered an injury. Sure, broken bones and lacerations may be obvious, but pain doesn't always show up right away.

When you're in a crash, your body goes into survival mode and starts pumping adrenaline through your body. Part of that adrenaline's job is to mask pain so you can deal with the threats in front of you.

You've probably seen football players on the spin bike between plays on the field. They do that because they have an injury, and the bike keeps their bodies from cooling down. So long as they keep the blood pumping and their hormones flowing, they won't register the hurt.

In the same way, your body may not feel its aches and pains—even serious ones–for a day or more. So, if you start feeling pain after the accident, don't delay in going to the doctor.

Gather Evidence If It's Safe

I would never recommend putting yourself at risk, but if you can safely gather evidence from your accident, get as much as you can.

Pull out that powerful evidence recorder in your pocket—your smartphone—and start taking pictures. Get pictures of all the vehicles involved. Then, take pictures of the street, obstructions, broken streetlights, and anything else that seems worth noting. If there's a traffic light issue, take a video of all the traffic lights as they change from green to yellow to red, all the way through. That way, your lawyer can see if they were malfunctioning or not.

Beyond that, get the names and phone numbers of any witnesses that are around. If someone says they saw something, your lawyer will want to talk to them, so make sure you can track them down.

Call an Attorney First

Many people think their first call after they call the police should be to their insurance. That may seem like the right thing to do, but I would caution against it.

You may think your insurance is on your side. They certainly cultivate that impression. The fact is, they want to minimize how much they pay for your care after an accident, and they'll use any method they can do to so.

Now, you will need to contact them within a few days of the accident, but your first call after you've looked after your health should be to a lawyer, not your insurance.

I've seen too many cases where the insurance company took advantage of people who weren't thinking straight. Your insurance adjuster may ask you something as seemingly innocent as, "are you okay?" That's a reasonable and common enough question, and your response, quite reasonably, might be, "Yeah, I'm okay."

In real life "I'm okay" means, "I haven't suffered any life-threatening injuries." But that answer could be used against you if you later say you had an injury. The insurance company will claim you told them you weren't hurt. Then, they'll try to avoid paying your medical bills.

Think about it like this: everyone knows from TV shows about the detectives that you don't talk to the police without a lawyer. That's a lesson well worth learning. As a deputy, I saw plenty of people who ended up in jail just because they waived their right to an attorney when they shouldn't have.

So, if you wouldn't talk to the police without a lawyer because you know you have to be careful what you say to the police, why would you talk to your insurance company without a lawyer?

Don't Sign Anything!

The insurance company won't just use your phone calls against you to limit their expenses. They'll use every trick they can think of.

Just look at what they did to Dave.

Dave was able to get full compensation, but only because he didn't sign anything. If he had placed his John Hancock on a check or an agreement, there wouldn't have been much we could do for him.

I've had to turn away far too many clients because they made that very mistake. It seems unfair, but that's just how the law works.

Insurance companies will use your ignorance of that fact against you. They'll give a check for a few thousand dollars and say, "this is for your hospital bill." They may even imply there's more to come. But as soon as you sign the back of that check, your claim is over.

So, don't sign anything from the insurance company until you talk to a lawyer. In fact, don't do anything with them. Insurance in Florida, as we are about to find out, is notoriously complicated, and after an accident, you don't want to be trying to navigate that system alone.

That's perhaps reason number one to go to a lawyer first.

Chapter 4

The Hybrid Insurance Monster

Six months ago, Brian Dirks was out riding his bike when he got hit by a car. Brian lived on this bicycle, and he had no other form of transportation. In fact, no one in his household had a car. If they couldn't bike, they walked or took the bus. Or, they stayed home.

So, when Brian got injured, he thought he was in a very bad situation. The injuries were significant—even if they weren't life-threatening—but he had no car insurance, since he had no car. Without that insurance, he had no idea how he was going to pay for his medical care.

When I found out no one in his household had vehicle insurance, I was very glad to be the one to deliver the good news. He was covered, but not in the way most of us are. Usually, our car insurance pays for our immediate medical needs. In Brian's case, though, the other person's personal injury protection (PIP) insurance would take care of him.

I didn't blame him for not knowing he was covered. It's a nuance of Florida law that rarely gets used. If a person is injured in an accident while either on foot or riding a non-motorized vehicle like a bike, and no one in their household has vehicle insurance, then they can use the coverage of the person who owns the car.

It's great that Florida provides that coverage, but the state's overly complex insurance system makes it hard to know when you're covered and when you're not. That's why I like to call this the Hybrid Insurance Monster.

This system is really difficult to navigate, but you are still responsible for understanding it. If you don't, insurance companies will use this complexity against you. In Brian's case, we had to go to bat for him and demand the insurance honor the driver's PIP coverage. They tried to wriggle out of responsibility, but we knew Brian's rights.

And I want you to know your rights, too.

Splitting Your Coverage

Florida doesn't make insurance easy. Instead of a single policy that either covers all of your medical and property damages or a policy that covers anyone who has been hit, we have a hybrid system that gives us a little of everything. We call this system No-Fault Insurance.

To begin with, the coverage is split between medical and property coverage. The state minimum is $10,000 of personal injury protection—which is a fancy way of saying medical coverage for you. That makes Florida a quote-unquote "No-fault state," but we'll soon see that the term is misleading.

The other half of the state statutory requirement is $10,000 of property damage coverage, but this doesn't cover your car, it covers repairs to the other person's car if you were responsible for the crash.

So, your insurance is there for *your* medical bills and for the *other person's* car repair.

Confused yet? Don't worry, we're just getting started.

The "Full Coverage" Myth

You may feel that a lot of this complexity has nothing to do with you. After all, you've got full coverage. You may not know what that means or how it works now, but you're confident you're covered, whatever happens.

A lot of people who come into my office feel that way. They believe that they should be fine because their insurance agent used that term.

However, that term is highly misleading in Florida. When an insurance agent says your coverage is "full," they usually meant "minimal." "Full" in this case means those statutory minimums I just laid out above.

$10,000 for PIP. $10,000 for property damage.

...And that's it.

"Full coverage" doesn't include any extras. There's no bodily injury protection (which covers the other person's injuries if you cause an accident). There's no collision coverage (which pays for repairs to your car after an accident). There's no uninsured motorist protection (which covers your medical bills and pain and suffering if the person who caused your accident has no or limited insurance coverage).

Far too often, I have to be the one to break it to my clients that "full coverage" doesn't provide any of the extras they assumed were in place.

So, don't make that assumption. Double check your insurance now so you know exactly what is covered. And get whatever extra coverage you can afford. You'll be grateful for it if you are ever in an accident.

Medical Bills: From No Fault to Fault

Many people assume their health insurance covers their medical expenses after an accident, but it's actually their car insurance that pays the bills…or at least part of them.

As I said above, the minimum PIP coverage is $10,000 in Florida. That covers 80% of your medical bills up to $10,000, minus any deductible.

But let's say your medical bills are $20,000. How are you going to get the rest of that bill covered?

That's when Florida stops being a no-fault state. As soon as your PIP coverage runs out, we flip a legal switch and look at who is at fault in the crash. The insurance of the at-fault driver will have to cover the rest of the medical bills, up to the limit of their policy.

Property Damage

Medical coverage is complicated enough, and we haven't even looked at your car yet.

Unless you have collision coverage (which you really should get), property damage goes through the at-fault driver's insurance only.

Now, that $10,000 minimum might sound like plenty after your accident, but that's only in an ideal scenario. If you're involved in a five-car crash, for instance, that $10,000 will be split between all the vehicles, meaning you'd only get $2,000 from that policy.

That's where your collision coverage would kick in, if you have it. In my experience, that coverage tends to get the job done on your car, and it goes quite a bit faster than other insurance compensation.

If don't have collision coverage, the rest of those repair bills will likely come back to you.

Going for Assets

Let's say you've been in an accident, and you're medical bills total $200,000. Unfortunately, the person who hit you only had $25,000 in bodily injury coverage. Normally, that would be the limit of what you could recover.

But that assumes the person doesn't have any assets. Assets include property and investments that can be sold to pay your bills when the other person is responsible for your injuries.

When we get a case, one of the first things we do for our clients is run background checks on the at-fault drivers to see if there are assets we can potentially recover if the insurance isn't enough.

We have a client right now who was rear-ended, and we've discovered that at-fault driver had bare minimum coverage but has significant assets.

We are now confident that, while the policy limit won't cover our client's bills, the assets of the driver who's carelessness harmed him will.

Why a Lawyer Is Helpful

One of the biggest complicating factors when you're dealing with all the hybrid insurance monster is that the insurance industry doesn't exist to help you. If they can convince you to take less for your property damage or your medical bills, they will. If they can confuse you enough that you don't receive the compensation you're entitled to, they will.

That's why it's helpful to get a lawyer involved from the beginning of the process.

We handle your medical and property claims all at the same time, removing the complexity and wait on your end. We do the background work—investigating the crash, getting the experts, and finding out how much compensation is available—so that you can focus on listening to your doctors and getting healthy again.

We take care of the tough stuff, so you can focus on hitting your recovery out of the park.

Part II

Hitting It Out of the Park

Chapter 5

What Makes the Value of My Case?

Rick Chase was one of our most recent clients. He is a motorcyclist who had been in a serious accident. The person who hit him had only a basic Florida policy, and Rick came to us with $50,000 in medical bills.

We took a deep dive into the defendant's assets, and we discovered that while he had a few modest investments, he'd lost the majority of them in a divorce dispute.

To get anything for Rick, we had to go through the whole litigation process. Through a lot of wrangling and legal work, we were able to get $10,000 on top of the full $10,000 in insurance coverage.

Despite the defendant's assets, $10,000 was the limit of what we could get. Rick appreciated that work and the extra compensation. It wasn't enough for his bills, but it made a difference.

At our firm, we pride ourselves on always being upfront about what your expectations should and shouldn't be on each case. Most people who come into our office have no idea what their case is worth, or if it's worth anything at all.

Knowledge is always your most powerful ally after an accident, and knowing more about the value of your case can help you prepare for what is ahead.

$100,000 Policy ≠ $100,000 Payout

A settlement is not dependent on a policy limit. We've already seen that, sometimes, we can get compensation outside the insurance limits by recovering assets. But it also works the other way. Even if a person has a massive policy, that doesn't mean the injured party is entitled to every cent.

The value of a case truly lies in how hurt you are. The more hurt you are, the more value your case has. The less hurt you are, the less value it has.

A $100,000 policy may lead to a $100,000 payout, but only if your injuries are significant. If you need back or neck surgery, for instance, you may be entitled to the full policy amount. If you only have a few aches and pains and a couple days off work, it will be significantly less.

You Won't Retire Off This... If You're Lucky

We've all read the stories of multi-million-dollar payouts after an accident. I understand it's tempting to almost hope for such compensation after an accident.

Those payouts, though, are the result of catastrophic injuries and, very often, deaths. It's important to realize that you don't want to have a case with a huge payout. This isn't the lottery. That money comes from horrific pain and suffering.

The goal in your case is not to make you rich. The goal is to make sure you are compensated for every dollar you spend on your care, plus all your time, effort, energy, pain, and suffering.

My aim as a lawyer is to make sure my clients don't lose a dollar of their own money or their potential income because someone else acted recklessly.

6 Ways We Determine the Value of Your Case

If a case isn't designed to deliver a massive payout regardless of the circumstances, how do we figure out what your claim worth?

To reach a value, we look at six aspects of your case:

- Past medical bills
- Future medical bills
- Past lost wages
- Future lost wages
- Past pain and suffering
- Future pain and suffering

Your past medical bills are the most straightforward part of the case. This is simply the total cost of all your treatment from the date of the crash to a specified date and time, such as the date we go to trial.

Future medical bills is more speculative, but it's what medical experts expect your future treatments to cost.

Your past lost wages account for all the time you were out of work due to your injuries. Meanwhile, your future lost wages—or, as we refer to it, future loss of earning capacity—is a little more complicated.

For those in very serious accidents, there may be a permanent reduction in their ability to work. Let's say my client worked as a manager at Chipotle before their accident. In that position, they made $20 a hour. After the accident, they can no longer stand for multiple hours, meaning, they can't return to that job.

Instead, they now have to take a job where they sit, but the only sitting jobs that they qualify for only pay $10 an hour.

The future loss of earning capacity addressing the pay gap between their former $20 an hour job and their future $10 an hour job. We look at that loss over a lifetime of work and try to get full compensation for the loss.

Past and future pain and suffering are the most difficult categories to calculate. With past pain and suffering, we use a minimum wage calculation. We tally up all the hours of treatment a client goes through and multiply that by the minimum wage. Then we ask the defense or the jury if they feel that amount would make it worth all the pain our client has gone through?

The obvious answer is "no."

We do the same thing with potential future pain and suffering, only we cut the wage in half and speculate on the number of hours the person will be in severe pain each day.

This process makes the pain and suffering more concrete and puts a figure on compensation.

Is My Case Big Enough?

Whether your case will hit seven figures or four, I want you to know that your case has value so long as it has value to you.

There's no perfect size for a case. A case is really dependent on the person who has been injured. Unlike some larger law firms, I never turn clients away just because the potential value of a case doesn't hit a particular figure. Whether your injuries will stay with you for life or you only require a couple doctor's visits.

It all comes down to you and how you feel about your case. When you come into my office, I'll sit you down and talk about the pros and cons going forward. We'll talk about the process, the expenses, the potential value. Then, I'll let you make the call.

I don't believe in turning away people who need help. I want you to come to me because I know just how much value a lawyer can add to your case. This has been proven in studies, but I don't need the studies to show me that. I see it every day.

Let me give you an example. We currently have two clients who were on a Hillsborough County transit bus that was in an accident. There are seven other claimants on that case in addition to our two, and there is only $20,000 coverage for everyone.

You might think that means everyone is going to get about $2,000 for their injuries, but the law doesn't work that way. In reality, in this case, my clients got 2.5 times the amount that the person without an attorney received. The reason for that is lawyers like me know the law and know how to fight for a better result. When you try to handle it alone, you expose yourself to the risk of receiving far less compensation than is available.

In other words, if you've been in any kind of accident, no matter how serious, you'll need a lawyer. Which means, you'll need to find the right lawyer for you.

Chapter 6

The Three Strikes against Personal Injury Lawyers

On occasion, I represent professional athletes in their contract negotiations. It's a way to stay connected to my sporting roots. And a few years ago, my firm represented a NASCAR driver. We were looking for advertisers, and I knew the head of a large law firm, who was a big racing fan.

More than that, I actually had a personal connection to this lawyer. Beyond a shared profession, my family knew his family. So, naturally, I contacted him to see if he would be interested in the opportunity.

I called his office, and when I didn't hear back, I texted his personal number. Then, I emailed him. He's a busy man, so I didn't expect a huge response—or even an immediate response—but I did assume he'd at least tell me "yes" or "no."

I never heard back from him.

Whenever I think of that story, I wonder how the clients at his firm ever get hold of their lawyers. If a colleague with a personal relationship and profitable opportunity can't get hold of the head of the firm—the man whose face is on all of their advertising—I don't have much hope for his clients.

When you are looking for a lawyer to represent you, it's important to realize that the commercials a big law firm puts out are designed to tell you a story. On TV, you see an incredibly successful and experienced lawyer who says he or she wants to represent you. They look right at you through the screen and tell you they care and they know how to win your case.

In reality, if you go to one of those big law firms, you will very likely never meet the lawyer you saw on the screen. Your case will go to a lawyer you've never heard of, with a record you know nothing about, and then you'll likely struggle to remain in contact with them.

This isn't hypothetical. Over and over again, clients have walked into my office after they started their case at a large law firm. They were convinced by the commercials, the name recognition, or a personal recommendation, but once they got there, they found that no one cared about their case. No one stayed in contact. No one updated them. No one put their interests first.

When you've been injured in an accident, you don't want to be in that position. You shouldn't have to switch attorneys midway through you case because you made the wrong choice upfront.

So, avoid making the wrong choice first by knowing what to look for the first time. Use these three strikes to find out if the firm you are considering has your interests at heart.

And with this system, it's one strike, and they're out.

Strike One: No One's on the Phone

First things first, find out when you speak to a law firm what guarantees they have about staying in contact. Any firm that really puts their clients first will have a system in place to ensure contact is regular and their clients are always up-to-date.

Those systems look different at different firms, but your primary goal is to get some kind of commitment about regular contact. And check the reviews online for the firm to ensure they live up to those commitments.

Strike Two: One Size Fits All Firms

Large firms in particular can be what I call numbers-based instead of client-based.

I am aware of a number of the most widely-known firms in Florida have, at least in the recent past, had trial quotas in place for all of their lawyers. That means, lawyers would push cases to trial just because they had to go to trial a certain number of times a year. It wasn't about the case, the client, or the defendant. If they needed a court date, they were going to get one, even if the outcome was worse for the accident victim.

This can be an incredibly risky strategy. Once a case goes to trial, it leaves the realm of the strictly legal and becomes about presentation.

I've witnessed a trial in which the injured party had hundreds of thousands of dollars in medical bills. The defendant and his lawyer, though, were very clever. They admitted fault and apologized. Then, they said they felt so bad, they felt the victim deserved $25,000 in compensation.

And that's just what the jury gave them. It barely made a dent in those bills, but the defendant came off as sympathetic, and that left the victim in serious debt.

Of course, sometimes, the only option is to go to trial, but that choice should be made by the client and only when the circumstances require it.

To ensure this doesn't happen to you, you'll have to take a more active role in your case. Make your feelings known from the outset and ask pointed questions about why a lawyer wants to pursue a certain strategy.

Strike Three: All-in-One Firms

As I mentioned at the top of this chapter, on very rare occasions, I represent professional athletes in their contract negotiations. I do that as a way to honor my past and remain a small part of the sports community. My day-to-day work—and my passion for law—all revolve around personal injury cases.

I believe that specializing in one area of law is critical to providing good service to clients. Law is complicated, and when you try to do it all, you end up doing none of it well.

Unfortunately, many law firms set themselves up to grab whatever kind of case they can. They do personal injury, and family law, and criminal law, and real estate law, and business law. They do everything. If someone has a case, they'll take it, whatever it is, and they'll figure it out as they go.

You want somebody who specializes in the area of law that is affecting you, because the lawyers on the other side are almost certainly specialists.

So, before you ever go to a law firm, take a look at the kinds of cases they advertise for. Do they claim to take care of everything? Then, it's probably best to go to a lawyer who focuses on your case instead.

The Easy Money Philosophy

All three of these strikes are tied together by a single philosophy that is far too pervasive in the legal world: easy money at all costs.

Many lawyers will take personal injury cases not because they care about helping their clients but because they think it's easy money. These lawyers will contact you as little as possible, push the case in one direction or the other—toward trial or toward an early settlement—and take every case that comes in the door if they think it will be "easy" on their end.

Your priorities in the case are always lower than their priority to get paid with the minimum work. I wish I was making this up, but unfortunately, I know plenty of lawyers who fit this description. Some of them are really great individuals outside the law office, but I'd never recommend their legal services to a friend.

These lawyers are particularly eager to take accident cases because they think they are the easiest to handle. I don't know how they got that idea. When we take a personal injury case, we monitor everything: we're in constant communication with doctors and experts; we're constantly reviewing medical records; we're constantly keeping an eye on the bills as they come in; we're constantly communicating, advising, and listening to our clients. It's non-stop work if you want to do it right. I suspect these lawyers aren't interested in doing it right.

And that shows in the results. Recently, we had a case in which a minor child was injured slightly in a case accident. The child went to two chiropractor appointments. The case was worth about $1,000.

Now, lawyers eager for a trial might have pushed for much more and received nothing, and lawyers eager to settle might have taken $1,000 or a little less just to move on.

Instead, we started out asking for $10,000, and because the adjusters knew us to be a tough, fair, hardworking firm, they called us up and offered $6,500. Because we do things right, we were able to provide that family with more than enough to cover all their accident-related expenses.

Law Firms Are Like Steakhouses

This may seem an odd comparison, but when I think of law firms, I think of steakhouses.

Some firms are of the cheap, quick, low-quality variety. They're like getting a steak sandwich at McDonald's. Sure, it's technically steak, but you don't expect much from it. In fact, it'd be a stretch to call such firms "steakhouses" in any sense.

Other firms are large and set up to follow certain rules, regardless of the specifics of the case. These firms are like Outback Steakhouse. At Outback, there's a chef somewhere who came up with the recipes, and each steak is expected to follow those recipes. There's little variety or uniqueness between the different platters.

Now, I'm Italian, and I was brought up to approach cooking far differently. Each meal was meant to be unique. I cook like my grandmother used to cook, where measurements are just a guide and not an absolute. You get a pinch of this, a dash of that. You throw something in, you taste it, and then you make adjustments to make that specific steak delicious.

That's the sort of service you expect at Bern's here in Tampa. Bern's has an in-house chef who adjusts recipes and makes every meal an experience. At Bern's you get treated like royalty, and your expectations are always exceeded.

To me, that's the type of experience you should get at smaller firms dedicated to client-focused service. Your case is unique, and your lawyer should develop a strategy around your needs and expectations.

Lawyers Should Always Put Clients First

Whether you're a steakhouse fan or not, you should know that your case deserves a personal touch and true focus from your attorney. Your lawyer should always put your interests first.

If they don't, you risk losing more than a little of the compensation you need, you risk months of delay and potentially the whole value of your case.

Luckily, there are lawyers out there who will always put you first. There are law firms that believe in keeping you informed and letting you call the shots.

And in Tampa, there's at least one law firm where that's always true: Franchi Law.

Chapter 7

Why You Want Me to Swing for the Fences for You

Like I said in the last chapter, I'm Italian, and I grew up with a belief that if people mattered to you, you treat them like family. That isn't just true for my friends, my teammates, my coaches, and my fellow officers, it's true for my clients as well.

At my firm, we believe every client should have a personal relationship with us. I've kept the staff intentionally small here, with just three of us in the office. That way, every client gets to know everyone who will work on their case. When you come to Franchi Law, you know exactly who your lawyer will be, who will answer your calls, and who to address your questions to.

We've designed this law firm around a simple concept: what would we want from a law firm if we needed help? We'd want open communication. We'd want to feel like we were in control.

We'd want this over with as soon as possible. And above all, we'd want to be treated honestly by a lawyer we could trust.

And that is what we try to offer everyone who walks in our doors.

A System Designed for Open Communication

You can't create a bond of trust and comfort with a client if you don't offer them the ability to stay connected to their own case. That's why we've designed a whole communication system to ensure we are always in contact and you can always contact us.

To begin with, we make sure to touch base at least every month throughout a case. Sometimes, that contact may be even more frequent.

Sometimes, though, clients need to hear from us between those scheduled check-ins. That's why we put our specialized texting system into place. With this system, a client can text our firm through a unique number. We then respond as soon as possible to their questions or concerns.

Further, these texts are then added to their file, so I review every concern every time I review the case file, which is multiple times a month. That way, everyone is aware of what is going on, and we're able to remain up-to-date on the legal and personal end of every case.

Client-Driven Decisions

Communication is crucial, but it's only a part of how our client-focused philosophy comes together. Even more importantly than having open lines of communication, I believe in making sure the client always gets to make the big decisions in their case.

Unlike those firms we discussed in the previous chapter, at Franchi Law, we don't predetermine what should happen in your case.

When you come to us, I will lay out what I think the value of your case is and what strategy I think is best, but I'll also provide you with different options. If I think it's worth a certain amount and worth going to trial over, but you just want a quick settlement and to move, then we settle, and you move on.

If I feel the case isn't strong enough for trial, but you're willing to risk it, then I go to the mat for you.

It's that simple. It's your show. I'm not interested in biasing you towards one choice or another. I'll tell you what I recommend and tell you if it's clear-cut or not, and then, I'll let you decide what's best for you.

This is also how we approach your medical treatment. As we discussed Chapter 1, often, your own doctor may not be willing to treat your injuries after an accident. When you come to us, I will provide you with the names of doctors who will help, but I don't force you to go to one doctor. I give you the names of a few specialists, and then I let you research them and decide which one is best for your treatment.

If you want more treatment options, I work to find more options. If you want more legal options, I look for more legal options. While I'm here to hit your case out of the park, I make sure you're always the one up to bat.

The Speed Your Case Needs

When you go to the one-size-fits-all firms, they'll put your case on a track, and it will take a set amount of time. Often, cases at those firms will last a year, maybe a year-and-a-half.

But since we specialize in treating each case as unique, at Franchi Law, we're often able to get results much faster. Those eighteen-month cases can sometimes be settled in as little as six months.

Of course, that doesn't mean we rush any cases. Some cases do require twelve months or more. Sometimes, there is significant treatment, which takes time. Sometimes, we do have to go trial, which takes time.

But the point is, we never put our timetable on your case. We will put in whatever time is needed, but you'll decide how fast you want to go and how big a priority speed is in your case.

We Keep It Honest and Let You Decide

Whether it's the potential settlement size, your medical options, or the speed of your case, I pride myself on being a straight shooter with every client. I will be completely honest with you. I don't believe in mincing words.

I won't promise a windfall when there's minor injuries and little property damage. And I won't promise a quick resolution if we're going up against a trucking company.

But once I've laid out the facts, I let you decide what happens next. That's my promise to you. In fact, it's one of several promises that I make to every client.

Chapter 8

Our Client Promise

I believe that we offer the best legal services to accident victims in all of Tampa, but getting that across can be difficult. There are plenty of firms taking up air space and billboards, pretending they care about their clients when they really care about their numbers.

That's why I developed our **Six Client Promises**. These aren't changes to our priorities, these are highlights of what we've always believed and always done at Franchi Law. These are six firm commitments we've always stood by, and which we will stand by with you.

If you walk into our office after an accident, we guarantee will fulfill all of these promises:

- Make sure you are updated regularly about the progress and status of your case
- Give you our opinion, good or bad
- Explain your legal rights and options in plain language
- Return your calls, emails, and texts in a timely manner
- You have the right to have your expectations exceeded by Franchi Injury Law
- You can terminate our representation (fire us) within 30 days of sign up for no fee if we fail to meet these promises

Regular Updates

We promise that you'll be updated on your case at least once a month, and often, more than that.

Those updates all depend on what is happening in the case. However, even when there's no progress over the course of a month, we'll still touch base to let you know what's going on and check in with how you're doing.

Our Honest Opinion

I'm always going to be honest with you about your case. I don't believe in misleading my clients.

Some lawyers who want to go to trial may tell you that your case could be worth far more than it realistically is. Others, who want to settle, may downplay the value. That will never happen in my office.

If I believe your case is worth $20,000, that's what I'll tell you, and then you can decide whether you want to settle for $15,000 or take the risk and go to trial to see if we can get far more.

The Law Explained in a Way You Understand It

The only way you can make the right decision for your case is if you understand exactly where you stand.

There's a lot of legal terminology and complex processes in an accident case. When a lawyer lays out your case using those terms, they may be talking to you honestly, but you'd never know it. They're almost speaking a foreign language.

That's never going to happen in my office. I'll walk you through the whole process using plain English. You can ask any question you want. The goal is for you to understand the prospects of your case as well as I do.

I do that because, again, I believe in putting you in the driver's seat for your case.

Constant Contact

We know already that some firms make it really hard to get someone on the phone and to get a question answered. At Franchi Law, that is never the case. With our text system and our personal relationship with our clients, we make sure to get back to you as quickly as possible with the answers you need.

Exceeding Your Expectations

I know that most people have fairly low expectations of lawyers, and I want to be part of what changes those feelings.

We never want a client to walk out of our office feeling like we didn't try hard enough or care enough about their case. In fact, we work hard to make sure every client feels the exact opposite. When you walk out of our office, you should not only feel like we care enough, but like we did everything possible to take care of you.

Fire Us If We Get It Wrong

The Florida Bar allows a law firm to charge a contingency fee if you stay with that firm for just three days. I think that's way too little time to know if your lawyer is doing their job right.

That's why we don't give you three measly days. We give you a month to make sure we're getting it done.

If, after a few weeks, you aren't happy with us, then I don't want your money. My chief concern is that you have the lawyer who will best represent your interests and get you the result you deserve after the trauma you've been through.

One Final Promise

There's actually one more promise I can make to you in these pages. Or rather, it's really the sum of the other six promises.

If you come to us, we'll do everything we can to take care of you and get you the compensation you need. We'll explore every option, review every potential strategy, and pursue every avenue you are comfortable with to make sure you can you can put your life back together as quickly as possible.

That's why I do what I do. That's why I'm here for you.

Conclusion

All I'm Asking for Is a Shot

I know what it feels like to be hurt and feel like life is never going to get back on track. An injury ended my baseball career. An injury ended my work as a deputy. {insert image 4}

In those tough times, I needed people I could trust and rely on to help me through the pain and the setbacks to return to the life I'd had before. That life was never quite the same again, but because of that assistance, it many ways, it was better.

My family, friends, coaches, teammates, and fellow deputies didn't give up on me, and that's why I'm committed to never giving up on a client, either.

When you're my client, you're never going to hear the words "there's nothing we can do" come out of my mouth. There are choices which may be more or less likely to succeed, but there's always something we can do together to try to set this situation right.

I recently had a client come to me desperate, saying they'd been to three different lawyers and no one wanted their case. Guess what? I took it, and we won.

You deserve a lawyer who takes a real interest in you and sees you as a person in a difficult moment, not a potential paycheck.

So, if you've been in an accident, and you need a lawyer who cares enough to give you the truth and do what it takes to take care of you, you can come to us.

After Coach Urso offered me a shot, I got injured, but I kept going. I got knocked down, and I got back up. That's the kind of commitment I'm offering you. You're down right now, and I know how to get you back on your feet.

You can call me today to discuss the details of your case. Whether you have a lawyer or not, I'm happy to answer any of your questions.

If you're just looking for more information to protect yourself and your family, follow our blog, like us on Facebook, and sign up for our newsletter.

You don't have to face this alone. You don't have to use a lawyer you can't trust.

You can get the compensation you need. You just need to give me a shot.

About the Author

William Franchi lives in Tampa with his wife and two boys. He is the proud founder of Franchi Injury Law, where he has recovered millions in settlements for his clients.

Tampa has been William's home since 2003. In 2006, he graduated from the University of Tampa with degrees in Sports Management and Criminology. After his short career as a deputy sheriff in the Pinellas County and Hillsborough County Sheriff's Office was ended by injury, William earned his law degree from Stetson University College of Law in 2012. He's been taking care of accident victims ever since.

William is proud to be a dedicated member of the Tampa community. He serves on the Alumni Board for the University of Tampa, and in 2018, he was awarded the University of Tampa's Alumni Achievement Award. In 2019, *Tampa Style Magazine* named him one of Tampa's Attorneys of the Year.

When out of the office, he enjoys spending time with his family and friends, boating the waters of Tampa Bay, golfing, and working out.

FRANCHI
INJURY
LAW

Made in the USA
Monee, IL
04 November 2026

67387231R00046